A Magical Homeschool: Nature Study

*52 Wonderful Ways to Use Nature Studies
in Every Season
to Teach Science, Math, Art and More*

By Alicia Bayer

Dedicated to my husband, Daryl,
and our children,
Victoria, Rhiannon, Jack, Alex and Fiona,
who have made homeschooling
such a magical adventure.

Table of Contents

Introduction

Our Homeschool Family

We are a family of seven in rural Minnesota, near Walnut Grove of "Little House" fame. My husband, Daryl, and I have five children – Victoria, Rhiannon, Jack, Alex and Fiona.

I never considered homeschooling until our oldest child, Victoria, was a toddler and I met a woman online who homeschooled her five daughters. She described a "typical day" where one child was reading on the couch, one was testing soil from a peach farm across the street because she thought pesticides were contaminating groundwater, and another child was still asleep since she was up late watching a meteor shower.

I fell in love with the idea of a homeschool where our children could learn together and follow their passions and interests with an education filled with books, experiences and hands-on learning. I convinced my husband to let us try homeschooling Victoria just for the early years and promised we'd enroll her in school if she was "behind" by the end of kindergarten. We didn't even make it to the kindergarten years before he was sold and it was clear that homeschooling was going to be a perfect fit for us.

Homeschooling is very hands-on and fun in our family. We learn a lot through books, games, projects and passions.

Nature studies has always fit into that perfectly. Our kids have grown up bird-watching with their father, helping me in the garden, exploring local woods, "exploding" cattails in the fall and blowing on dandelions to make wishes. Over the years, we've expanded on this by learning foraging as a family, having weekly hiking days, experimenting with natural materials, adopting a wetland to keep clean and more.

Our oldest child, Victoria, has now finished her homeschooling years and is beginning college, while our youngest child, Fiona, has just begun. It is through activities like nature studies that this homeschool adventure has been so educational and rewarding all of these years.

I hope this book provides a bit of nature study inspiration for your homeschool family. Have fun!

~Alicia

Why Teach Nature Study?

Nature study can be an invaluable part of a child's homeschooling. Most parents know that kids enjoy nature study, but many don't realize the many ways it is vital for the best possible education.

1. It's an easy way to teach science. Children will quite easily learn scientific fields like biology, geology and even chemistry by observing and experimenting with nature.

2. It lays the foundation for higher learning. The more that children learn about the natural world, the more easily they will understand sophisticated scientific concepts later. When a child has created her own terrarium, for instance, she can quite easily understand concepts such as transpiration and ecosystems.

3. It gets the kids outside. We all know that children benefit from time in nature. It gives the entire family access to exercise, fresh air, sunlight and the mood-lifting benefits of time outside. Time in green spaces has even been found to reduce ADHD symptoms, and nature studies are a wonderful way to make that part of your homeschool routine.

4. It can be done anywhere. You don't have to live in the country to do nature studies. We all have weather. We all have access to plants, birds and insects. Nature studies can be done on rooftops and windowsills, in good weather and in bad, on sidewalks and empty lots.

5. It's free. You have an endless supply of absolutely free educational materials right outside your doorstep or window. Kids can observe and interact with everything from ants to weeds to snowflakes without costing you a cent.

6. It can help put the fun back into learning. Children may be bored by worksheets and textbooks but they will almost always get excited about the same subject if they get to participate in a hands-on way.

7. It works in other subjects. Kids practice handwriting and spelling while writing in nature journals. They use math while figuring out times, temperatures and growth rates (even by telling the temperature by cricket chirps!). They can even study history with nature studies through activities like planting a Native American "three sisters" garden, identifying fossils, or using natural materials to make tools and toys from the pioneer days.

8. It gives children a sense of stewardship for the earth. Nature study helps children understand and appreciate our role in taking care of our environment. They see firsthand how our actions influence the plants, animals, birds, water and world around us.

9. It develops critical thinking skills. When engaging in nature studies, children are not simply memorizing or passively learning. They are able to make connections and see science at work in ways that allow them to learn firsthand and become true scientists themselves.

10. Children find it magical. It's one thing to read about the life cycle of a frog, but it's quite another to go out and catch tadpoles. Activities like raising butterflies, collecting rocks, growing gardens, catching fireflies, starting nature journals and making snow candy are activities that give children a lifelong connection to nature — and make some pretty wonderful memories along the way.

Remember, nature studies don't have to be formal or complicated. You can start by simply committing to spending time outside for a half hour a day together — taking a walk, examining the parts of a wildflower, starting a backyard bird log, comparing roots on two kinds of weeds pulled from the garden....

Follow your child's lead and the rest is easy.

Getting Started in Nature Study

At its most basic, nature study simply involves setting aside time each day to spend either outside or inside with natural elements.

Charlotte Mason, a famous educator who has inspired many homeschoolers, taught that nature study should be a central part of every child's education. Charlotte Mason recommended taking children outside for nature study every day, if possible, and teaching them to use nature journals.

You can create a nature journal for your child with any blank sketch book, notebook or homemade book. Provide your child with pencils (for sketching and coloring) and watercolor paints if you like, too.

When you're on nature walks, ask your child to find an element of nature to sketch (such as a wildflower, bird's egg or insect) with as much detail as possible.

Help your child label the item with information such as its Latin name, common name and details about it. This can be done "in the field" with the help of an ID book or at home after looking it up.

Other common nature study practices involve activities such as:

* Feeding the birds

* Growing a garden

* Examining natural items up close (slicing open a red pepper to examine the seeds, watching a bee collect pollen from flowers, and so on)

* Reading books about nature

* Keeping an assortment of natural items like pine cones, shells, seed pods, fossils and dried flowers where children can study them, along with helpful items such as a magnifying glass and assortment of ID books.

About Our Nature Study Projects

Many people think of nature studies as just a few types of activities, such as sketching plants, observing birds and animals, and collecting natural items.

The activities in this book include that type of activity but also take advantage of all types of other opportunities that make use of the natural world around us, such as learning how to collect micrometeorites at the beach and how to turn your campfire different colors by adding different substances.

Traditional nature study activities generally fall into the biology division of science. You'll find that a lot of these activities also involve chemistry, astronomy, meteorology and other branches.

The projects in this book are designed to work for homeschooling families with a wide variety of ages. Some projects and activities are better suited for younger kids while others are best suited for older kids and teens, but most of the activities can involve all of the kids in one way or another -- after all, that's how most homeschool families operate!

Use your discretion to determine which activities are the best fit for your children.

You'll find blank nature journal pages at the end of each season's section and at the end of the book.

Families can use the seasonal pages to sketch natural items, make notes about projects and experiments, record observations, and more.

Seasonal pages include:

- Nature sketch pages for each season
- Nature project records and observations for each season

Year-round pages include:

- Bird sighting pages
- Animal sighting pages
- Garden/foraging records

About the Seasons in This Book

The nature study projects in this book are broken down into seasons, with 13 nature study ideas for each season (one for each week of the year).

Many of these projects can be done any time of year, and most of these can be done by families in any climate, though some of the projects involve materials such as snow or autumn leaves.

When possible, alternate suggestions are provided for those in climates that might not have access to these nature study materials.

Remember that the seasons are provided as a general guide to make the most out of each time of year, but feel free to use the projects at any time and in whatever order you like!

Spring Nature Study Projects

Spring is the perfect time for studying seeds, birds and baby animals. It is the season of new life and new beginnings. This is a great time for seed starting projects and tracking the return of migratory birds.

If your family does foraging, look for wild edibles such as ramps (wild leeks), morels, wild greens and wild asparagus at the end of the season.

Here are a few projects to make the most of spring.

Carnation Rainbows

This classic science experiment is a tradition for a reason. It quite simply shows kids how flowers transport water and is also just pretty!

Put white carnations in glasses of water tinted with various colors of food coloring and then watch over the next few days as the petals turn the colors of the water.

For a fun variation, split the stems on some and put half in one color of water and half in another. Also try the experiment with other items, such as celery stalks.

Soil pH Vinegar Test

It's important to know how acidic or alkaline your soil is to best meet the needs of your garden plants. Here's an easy way to use vinegar to test it, from This Old House:

"Place a handful of dirt into a small container and sprinkle vinegar on it. If it fizzes, the soil is alkaline; adjust the pH with an acid amendment."

Test soil from various parts of your yard and then test soil from other locations. Ask the kids to predict ahead of time whether the vinegar will fizz.

You can also purchase a more precise soil testing kit for a few dollars. If you do, see how the vinegar test compared in accuracy.

Naturally Dyed Homemade Play Dough

Making your own play dough is fast, easy and inexpensive. Using natural dyes adds to the fun and produces some beautiful, earth-friendly results.

We've been making our own play dough for years but we originally used artificial food coloring to tint it. We actually have a whole assortment of different colors of synthetic food dyes that we use just for craft recipes (we tint our foods with natural homemade dyes for health reasons).

Then, when my son Jack was seven years old, he and I began experimenting with dyeing our play dough with natural dyes and we were hooked. Not only are the resulting colors gorgeous, but there's a sense of experimentation and discovery when you create colors on your own. Also, using fewer petroleum-based products is always a good thing.

You can tint your dough with either dry powders (such as turmeric) or liquids (such as water that has been tinted with beets or berries).

Here's the basic recipe you use when making your own cooked playdough:

- 1/2 cup of flour (plus powders like turmeric, if using)
- 1/2 cup of water (colored with natural materials, if using)
- 1/4 cup of salt
- 1/2 tbsp cream of tartar
- 1/2 tbsp cooking oil

Steps:

1. Combine all ingredients in a pan.

2. Cook over medium heat, stirring constantly, until mixtures thickens into a ball and pulls away from the sides of the pan (about five minutes).

3. Allow to cool slightly and knead.

This recipe makes a small amount (slightly more than an average container of purchased play dough), the perfect size for one color or one child.

You can make individual batches for each color you'd like or double it to make lots of one color and then tint half of it with a new color after cooking. For example, for one set of colors Jack and I made a batch with beet juice to make pink, then we took half of it and worked in a half teaspoon of turmeric powder to make orange.

Here are some materials to try for natural colors:

Turmeric powder (found in the spice aisle of grocery stores) produces a bright gold and mixes well to make secondary colors. A little goes a long way! Try a half teaspoon to start.

Beets make a beautiful deep pink. Use beet powder, simmer a sliced beet in water for a few minutes, or just use some juice from pickled beets mixed with water.

Blueberries can be simmered in water, crushed and put through a sieve for purple-blue.

Crabapples can be simmered in water, reduced by cooking and strained for a beautiful red-pink.

Cherries, strawberries and other berries can be similarly cooked to make red.

Concentrated juices such as grape can make purple and other colors.

Brewed coffee can be used for the liquid to make tan.

Walnut bark can be simmered and strained to make dark brown.

Spinach can be simmered to produce green.

Artichokes make gorgeous green-blue water when you simmer or pressure cook them for teal.

Experiment with lots of colors and types of foods!

A note on scents: Some of these materials (such as turmeric) have strong scents. If you like, you can mix in a few drops of an essential oil to counterbalance it and create a soothing or fun scent. Kids can also enjoy the wide variety of different scents, however, and this adds to the educational value.

Preservation: We keep our play doughs in covered containers in the fridge. It keeps well for us, though it doesn't have to last more than a couple of weeks with the amount of use it gets with our kids before we're making new.

Edible Flowers

There are all kinds of flowers that are edible, from dandelions to tulips to violets.

Research the edible flowers in your area with the kids and find some recipes to try.

Be sure to only use flowers that have been grown organically and not sprayed with pesticides. Flowers from florists and garden centers are not safe to consume.

Here are some ideas for ways to sample edible flowers.

- Chop dandelion flowers (just the yellow parts and not the bitter white part that connects them) and stir them into pancake or muffin batter.

- Serve mousse in tulips.

- Put alliums (the flowering tops of garlic and onions) on top of soups or salads.

- Try making candied violets or violet syrup (which is also a pH indicator and will turn colors when you add lemon juice!).

- Grow colorful nasturtiums from

seed in your summer garden. The leaves and flowers are all edible, and look beautiful in salads. They have a peppery flavor.

These are just a few of the flowers that are edible and just a few ways to use them.

Of course, grocery store foods such as broccoli and artichokes are also flowers!

Remind kids to always be 100% positive on plant identification before eating any plant, and also try new plants in small quantities in case of allergy (as is the case with any new food).

Micro Sketches

Have the kids take a magnifying glass, pocket microscope or Brock Magiscope outside, along with a nature journal or notebook. Challenge them to look at 5 things each day close up this month and draw what they see.

They can label their finds with as much detail as they like (for more sophisticated nature studies, consider details like Latin names, families, facts, etc.).

For a fun extension, have them cover the names of their items and see if others can guess what they are.

Tip: Pocket microscopes are small, hand-held magnifiers that come with a small light. They are remarkably inexpensive and fabulous for nature studies. You can find them on eBay, Amazon or American Science and Surplus.

Valentines Chocolate Box Rock Collection

Spring is a great time to start a rock collection with each child. Empty chocolate boxes from Valentine's Day are fabulous containers to use to start your child's collection.

Use a rock ID book or an online guide to try to label each type of rock on the inside of the container.

Any time you go on a vacation, put aside some time to look for new specimens for your child's collection. The types of rocks in the environment vary greatly from place to place, even in the same state.

Making The Wind

Place a balloon over the mouth of a plastic water bottle. Pour a few inches of very hot water into a cup. Set the water bottle in the hot water. After a few moments, the balloon will stand straight up as the air inside the bottle warms and expands into the balloon.

Explain that as the sun warms air around the earth, the air rises. Colder air then moves in to fill the vacant spot. What is moving air called? Wind! This is why whenever the weather suddenly heats up much more than it has been, we tend to get windy weather right after.

Extend this activity by hanging wind socks or weather-proof streamers outside where the kids can observe the wind speed outside. See if they can notice any patterns in terms of wind and weather.

Temperature studies

Give the kids a thermometer (digital thermometer "guns" are especially fun!) and have them measure the temperature outside, inside and in various parts of the house.

How much hotter is it in the full sun than the shade?

How much cooler is it in the basement?

What about the attic?

Challenge them to guess the absolute coldest place on your property, along with the warmest, and then have them take measurements to see if they were right. Have them figure out the difference and why they think some places are so much cooler or warmer.

Color-Changing Purple Cabbage Water

Here's a fantastic science experiment that teaches children about the pH scale in a nearly magical way.

This is one of those science experiments that's extremely educational but also so much fun that it keeps kids (even little ones) occupied and happy for quite some time!

When steeped in boiling water, purple cabbage creates a deep purple liquid that you can use to test the pH of different liquids and substances.

It reacts by changing colors, from vivid hot pink for acids to blue and even green for bases. You can even get it to turn clear (the kids will have to experiment to figure out how!).

Before beginning the experiment, talk to your kids a little bit about the fact that the pH scale measures things like acids and bases. Discuss pH while you experiment with the substances — how shampoo is supposed to be pH balanced so it doesn't sting eyes, how some hydrangeas are pink in acidic soil and blue in alkaline, and so on.

One of the nice things about this experiment is that you can use non-toxic substances like vinegar, lemon juice and baby shampoo to do it with younger kids. Older kids will enjoy testing additional substances, such as alum and laundry detergent, in order to see a wider range of results (and colors).

You'll need:

- One small head of purple cabbage
- A pan with a lid
- Water
- One light colored ice cube tray or mini muffin pan per child (or a series of small glass bowls)
- Eyedroppers, tiny spoons and/or pipettes
- A variety of substances to test for pH -- see suggestions in step 4 and use substances that are safe to use around your children
- Small dishes for your substances

Steps:

1. Chop about 2 cups of purple cabbage and cover with boiling water. Put a lid on it and steep for about 10 minutes.

2. Strain out the liquid and reserve. It should be a deep blue-purple color, though it may be affected somewhat by your water.

3. Put a little cabbage water in each compartment of a light colored ice cube tray or similar container with many sections. For little kids, a muffin tin works well.

4. Assemble a variety of substances (preferably white or clear) to test and pour a little of each into a container. Some options are: hot sauce, white wine, lemon juice, witch hazel, alcohol, different types of shampoo, fingernail polish remover, hydrogen peroxide, laundry detergent, baking powder, alum, salt, club soda, apple cider vinegar, baking soda and control of purple cabbage water with nothing added.

5. For younger kids, put just a few in some larger dishes and aim for

nontoxic ingredients like vinegar and baking soda.

6. Give each child a small spoon and an eye dropper and explain about the pH scale and how the color will change (more pink for acidic, more towards green or almost yellow for base).

7. Let the kids add various substances and see what happens! Make sure you keep track of which substance was added to which compartment.

Some of the best reactions we've made were from alum, hydrogen peroxide, hot sauce (2 drops and it was hot pink!), wine and club soda.

You can also use the purple cabbage water to compare rainwater (or melted snow) to tap water to distilled water, in order to determine if there's a difference in pH value for water from different sources.

But wait, there's more! Once you've changed the colors of the liquid in each, challenge the kids to change it back! Ask them to think about what they can add to a hot pink to make it blue again, for instance. In a few cases, you end up with a reaction (notably baking soda and vinegar ending up in one compartment).

Seed Starting

This is the time to get a start on that summer garden with vegetables that need a big head-start.

You can find garden planning calendars and seed starting charts to make it easy.

Go through seed catalogs and plan days to germination, days to harvest, garden placement and more.

If you don't have room for a garden outside, you can still start seeds for container gardening. Even a sunny windowsill or balcony can work for container gardening.

Project Noah

Use the free Project Noah app to log and ID bugs, birds, seeds and more. This wonderful Citizen Scientist app can be used in all sorts of fun ways.

Spottings can be added to "missions", such as "Birds of the World" or "Global Urban Biodiversity." Kids can take part in "BioBlitz," where participants identify and count all the organisms found in a given area, like Rocky Mountain State Park. Kids can also create their own missions.

Other tools on the website and app include a map on which you can search for spottings in your local area or by types of organisms. Kids can learn from spottings that are posted all around the world. Families can also share spotting via Facebook or Twitter, plus connect with friends that are also also using Project Noah.

Worm Calling

Find an area with loose, slightly moist dirt, such as under a log or landscape timber and push a 12 to 18 inch stick a few inches into the ground. Rub another stick vigorously against that stick for several minutes and watch what happens. If there are worms in the area, they should wriggle to the surface.

You can try this in several areas of the yard to see which ones seem to be the best worm hang-outs.

Scientists aren't sure why this brings worms to the surface, but they think the vibrations made by rubbing the sticks together may mimic those of natural predators, and they come up to the surface to escape.

Bird Nest Supply Cages

Use suet cages to put out lots of varieties for birds to build their nests from, such as short lengths of yarn and even hair from your hair brushes or pet fur.

Scraps should be trimmed to lengths of 3-8 inches to be most useful to the birds. If they're any shorter, they can't be used for nest construction, and any longer and they pose a threat of tangling, which can cause strangulation.

Birds can have preferences for certain types of yarn (such as natural and synthetic) and even for colors. Watch to see which ones your local birds like best and see if you can spot your family's colorful yarn in nests in the coming months!

Spring Nature Sketches

Spring Nature Sketches

Spring Nature Projects & Observations

Spring Nature Projects & Observations

Summer Nature Study Projects

Summer is the perfect time for garden projects and trips to the beach. This is a great time for weather watching, cloud watching and outdoor adventures.

If your family forages, look for wild edibles such as raspberries, blueberries, crab apples, wild pears and stinging nettles (careful!) this time of year.

Be sure to continue your nature studies on family vacations to other geographic areas, where you can find new-to-you species of birds and animals, along with lots of new natural materials to collect.

Here are some nature study projects well suited for summer.

Ant Science

It's summertime and that means the ants are making pests of themselves around some homes. Why not take advantage of their presence to do some fun educational projects outside?

From ant mazes to taste tests (for the ants, not the kids!), here are some fun projects involving some of nature's hardest workers.

Make an ant maze! When my oldest daughter was 12, I mentioned to her that chalk lines are supposed to keep ants out of houses, since they supposedly don't like to cross them. Victoria decided to test that hypothesis with some chalk and she drew some lines around some ants in the driveway. Sure enough, one little one turned around and went the other way when faced with a chalk line. Victoria took it a step further by drawing a maze around several of them with some sugar as a lure at the end, and they ran it! The ants will cross the line if they have to, but for the most part they stayed in the lines for us.

Test natural repellents. Along with chalk, there are many other substances that are supposed to naturally repel ants. Find a list of natural repellents online and try a few of the safer ones. Find some ants and put down a variety of the substances to see which ones they really seem to avoid. Have the kids guess ahead of time which substances they think will work best and then see how right they are.

Have a taste test. Have the kids put out a variety of treats they think the ants will like, and see which ones they seem to favor. Again, have the kids hypothesize ahead of time which foods the ants will prefer. Ask the kids if they think ants are herbivores, carnivores or omnivores, and put out foods to test their opinions. The nice thing about working with ants is that you only need tiny amounts, too!

Make a paper trail. Explain to the kids that ants leave a scent trail to communicate with other ants. Once you find a line of ants going in one direction (towards one of your food sources, for instance), put a piece of paper in the path and wait for the ants to establish a trail across it. After they've done so, turn the paper and watch what happens.

Finding Meteorites!

Every so often, my husband takes our kids to a nearby lake to look for meteorites. Yes, meteorites! Okay, they're micrometeorites to be more specific, but nonetheless, the kids are able to find and hold something that came from millions of miles away in space. Can you think of a cooler way to spend a Wednesday afternoon?!

What's a micrometeorite and why are they on the beach? Pieces of rock and metal are constantly colliding with Earth's upper atmosphere. Most of these are walnut-sized or smaller, traveling at tens of thousands of miles per hour. The upper atmosphere is very thin, about 50 to 62 miles, but it creates enough friction that they heat up to temperatures that make them burn very brightly. These are meteors, although people often call them "shooting stars."

Most meteors burn up completely in the atmosphere. Those that survive and fall to Earth are called meteorites. About 30,000 tons of "space matter" is deposited on Earth each year. This is composed of bits of comets, chunks of asteroids and debris from the formation of our solar system long ago. Most of this material falls into the oceans, and most of the rest that reaches us is microscopic, too small to be noticed.

These tiny pieces are known as micrometeorites. Tons of micrometeorites fall each year, all around us -- but we don't usually even know they're there.

There are lots of experiments online that recommend using rainfall, rooftops and visits to Antarctica to collect micrometeorites. Many involve waiting weeks (or an awfully long field trip). Since we're sort of an impatient family, we wanted to do something that would require a little less time and effort. Our way is not quite as scientific as an expedition to Antarctica, but it is a great way to spark excitement about science. -- And it involves hanging out at the lake, which is pretty nice too.

Note that you can do this in any wide open space outside. We use the lake, but a field will do. Avoid parking lots and areas that are likely to have a lot of man-made materials, though, or you're likely to pick up lots of magnetic substances that are slightly less cosmic!

Here's what you need: We use a large magnet "pick up tool" purchased inexpensively on Amazon but any strong magnet will do. This type is nice because you can pull the handle to release the magnetic pull. We also use a plastic sandwich bag, a string and a piece of white paper.

Here's what you do: Take the magnet, tie a string on the handle, and walk along, swinging the magnet just barely over the sand (and sometimes dragging it through it). After about 10 feet, go to the shore where you have a piece of white paper on the ground. Hold the magnet over the paper and pull the release, so the particles fall on the paper (sometimes you may have to scrape them off the side as well). Once all the collected materials are on the paper, fold it to make a pour spout and put them in a collecting bag.

If you don't have a pull-release magnet, simply put a strong magnet in a sandwich bag and proceed the same way. When you want to release the magnetic grains, simply hold the magnet in the bag over the paper and withdraw the magnet from the bag. The particles will then fall to the paper.

Why it works: Meteorites are most easily found in dry, desert regions. That said, tens of thousands of tons of meteorite dust fall every year all over the earth. These particles fall everywhere -- even in our back yards and at our lakes. Meteorites contain iron, which is magnetic. Earth rocks are not magnetic, though they can contain magnetic particles (and other particles you can find will be magnetic too, of course).

There are detractors out there who tell you that this type of experiment won't get only micrometeorites because other magnetic particles are out there, particularly from industrial pollution. That may be, and you can explain to the children that some of the magnetic particles will probably not be micrometeorites. But the fact is that some of them are, and that sort of fact is exactly the sort of fact that gets children really excited about astonomy.

Furthermore, this is a great dilemma to discuss with the children. Talk about how you might be able to tell the difference. Could you tell by looking at the particles under a microscope? Micrometeorites are supposed to be cyllindrical from their fall through the atmosphere. Some of the other types of magnetic particles would be and others would not. Are there any tests you could perform or other ways to identify the real micrometeorites from the imposters?

The book <u>We Dare You</u> talks about how to find meteorites at the beach (with similar instructions) and also gives instructions on how to harvest micrometeorites from rainwater in gutters if you're not near a beach.

The Dead Insect Society

Here's a nature study project that should be a staple in every homeschool. Collect some dead bugs and look at them together under a lighted pocket microscope or with a magnifying glass.

Look at the mouth of a dead horsefly (which resembles a beak!) under magnification and the kids will probably decide that it's no wonder their bites hurt so much.

If the kids like, they can start a collection and label their specimens (ID books can be great for this). Empty chocolate boxes make perfect holders for bugs, or use egg cartons or small plastic storage containers.

"Days of the week" pill containers work very well as carriers. Pop one in your bag when you head out on nature walks, and carefully transfer insects to the compartments as you find them.

Use tweezers to protect fingers from stingers and other dangerous parts.

Telling the Temperature with Crickets

Here's a great way to combine nature studies, science and math in a really fun way -- use crickets to tell the temperature.

My husband has been teaching our kids to tell the temperature by counting cricket chirps for years. It sounds like a bit of blarney, but it actually works and scientists have been using the trick since the late 1800's.

How does it work? Crickets, like all insects, are cold-blooded, which means they take on the temperature of their surroundings. There is a special equation called the Arrhenius equation that cold-blooded animals follow that determines things like the speed at which ants walk and the rate that crickets chirp.

All living things have many chemical reactions that go on inside their bodies. The Arrhenius equation describes the activation energy (or threshold energy) required to make a chemical reaction occur inside the organism. As the temperature rises, it becomes easier for chemical reactions in cold blooded animals to happen, so they happen more rapidly. Chemical reactions are needed to contract the muscles crickets use to chirp. As the temperature rises, the rates of the chemical reactions inside the crickets' bodies speed up, causing characteristics such as the chirping to also speed up.

The formulas differ slightly, depending on whom you ask.

The first cricket temperature formula was created by A. E. Dolbear in 1898. He studied various species of crickets to determine their chirp rate and then created Dolbear's Law: $T=50+[(N-40)/4]$ (with T representing temperature Fahrenheit and N representing number of chirps in 1 minute).

NOAA uses the simple formula of counting the chirps in 15 seconds and adding 40.

The Old Farmers' Almanac recommends another simple formula: To get a rough estimate of the temperature in degrees Fahrenheit, count the number of chirps in 15 seconds and then add 37.

To get the temperature in degrees Celsius, count the number of chirps in 25 seconds, divide by 3, then add 4.

Want to get even more precise? Dolbear and some other scientists determined that different species of crickets and katydids chirped at slightly different rates. They devised different formulas for each of these species (click on each name to see an up close picture and hear an example of that species' chirps):

Field Cricket $T = 50+[(N-40)/4]$

Snowy Tree Cricket $T = 50+[(N-92)/4.7]$

Common True Katydid $T = 60+[(N-19)/3]$

Challenge the kids to determine which variety of cricket is common in your back yard and see if the formula gets a more accurate temperature.

Be sure to tell the kids that (usually) only male crickets chirp, and usually only at night. There are actually several reasons why they chirp.

Scientists think that these reasons can be:

- Calling to attract a female with a a loud and monotonous sound

- Courting a nearby female with a quick, softer chirp

- Behaving aggressively during the encounter of two males

- Sounding a danger alert when sensing trouble

How do crickets chirp? Crickets make sounds by using a process called stridulation, where special body parts are rubbed together to make a noise. Crickets have a special structure on the top of their wings called a scraper. They raise their wings to a 45-degree angle (similar to the way we raise the lid on a piano to increase its volume) and draw the scraper of one wing across a series of wrinkles on the underside of the other wing, which is called a file. The process is somewhat like running your fingernail across the teeth of a comb, and it results in the characteristic chirping sound.

Weed Lab

If you have weeds in your yard (and who doesn't?), put them to use!

Help the kids dig up an assortment of similar weeds from the yard and pot them up. Then have the kids experiment with different types of light, amounts of water and treatments for each plant and see how they fare.

Try putting one in full shade and one in direct sun, mulch one with rocks leave the rest alone, water one with salt water, water one with tap water, let at least one get water only from rain, and so on.

Have the kids make hypotheses ahead of time about how they think each weed will do.

If they like, they can make a chart of the results.

What helped the weeds thrive?

What killed them off?

You can also extend this on a longer term by trying to prove or disprove health claims.

Will microwaved water really kill plants?

How will they fare on boiled water or

distilled water?

If you pour the cooking water from vegetables onto the plants regularly, will they grow better from the added nutrients?

What if you add common chemical food additives like food coloring or artificial sweetener?

What about salt?

Coconut Oil Thermometer

We all know that the melting point of ice is a chilly 33 degrees, but many pantry items have much higher melting points.

Coconut oil is a perfect example of this, with a melting point of 76 degrees.

Get a jar of coconut oil and have the kids put a small scoop on a saucer and take it to various parts of the house.

Is it solid or liquid?

What about if you take it outside?

Have the kids use what they know about its melting point to estimate temperatures in various spots and then see how close they get.

Remind them to give the oil time to adjust to the heat of each location, and also ask them if they can estimate how much warmer or cooler the temperature is than 76 degrees by how quickly the state of the oil changes.

If it's a really hot day, you can take the experiment further and use butter, which is said to melt at between 90 and 95 degrees.

Is there anywhere they can go where

butter will melt?

How much and how fast?

What would they estimate the temperature is at that location, judging by the butter's state?

This is a fun way to use science to take advantage of heat waves.

If it's hot enough to melt butter, you officially have permission to go find a fun place to cool off!

Foster Creatures

Summer is a great time to find an insect or other small creature to bring inside and care for in temporary, up-close nature studies.

Over the years, our family has temporarily housed quite a variety of creatures, from praying mantis babies to a wide variety of caterpillars to an injured field mouse.

We have provided habitats and food for dozens of monarch caterpillars (sometimes starting as eggs on milkweed leaves) that transformed into butterflies that we released in the back yard. We even had a crayfish from Plum Creek that lived in a tank on our kitchen counter for a while. She lived happily on fish food pellets and an assortment of treats such as lettuce.

Most of our visitors were short-term unless they were not able to survive in the wild. This is always the best way to treat wild creatures, since it is better for them and the ecosystem for them to live in their natural habitats.

Here are some creatures that are well suited for temporary (even an hour) adoption:

* Tadpoles

* Caterpillars

* Lizards

* Frogs and toads

* Praying mantises

* Crickets

* Fireflies

* Minnows

* Turtles

Before you collect a creature for nature study, be sure of the following:

* That you have a suitable, safe container for it to live in temporarily. This can be a fish tank, a plastic jug with a lid or even a large jar. Make sure there are air holes in your container that are large enough to let air in (if needed) but not so large that your creature can escape.

* That you have properly identified your creature ahead of time and know what it is, what it eats and what it needs to survive -- and that you can provide all of that, if necessary. For instance, our kids once found a crecopia caterpillar in a parking lot and wanted to take it home to care for it. We used our cell phone to

google what it was and what it ate. When we found out that one of its preferred foods was cherry leaves, we decided we could bring it home because we have a cherry tree in our yard.

 * That your creature is not protected or endangered.

 * That your creature is safe to study (something like poisonous spiders and scorpions are not wise specimens!).

 * That you are able to bring your creature back to the same area where you caught it.

Remind children not to handle the creatures with bare hands. This is for everyone's protection. Some creatures bite, sting or spread diseases such as salmonella. Handling them can also cause many creatures great stress, as they will rightly think of children as predators.

Also remind them to be gentle and considerate to the temporary pets.

Sand Study

If you look online, you can see photos of beach sand that show the amazing beauty and variety of grains of sand when they're magnified.

Head to area spots and collect sand of your own to view under the microscope and see what your area sands look like.

If you have any sand from vacations, compare that to your local sands. Ask the kids if they predict a difference in sands from places like rivers, lakes and even playgrounds, and then see how they compare.

If they like, have them sketch the way sand from several different locations looks when it's magnified.

The Tomato Test

Organic and naturally grown tomatoes are said to have far more nutrients and mass than commercially grown tomatoes. Here's a way to put that to the test.

One organic grower said that he purchased a few tomatoes at the supermarket to use as a comparison with his organic tomatoes for customers who visited his gardens. He selected a few of his vine-ripened tomatoes that were the exact same circumference, proven by tape measurement, and weighed them all on carefully calibrated scales. He said that his tomatoes were 15-20% heavier than the "hollow" commercial tomatoes. He said that sometimes he would put one of each into the hands of a customer and ask them which was heavier. They always selected the organic tomatoes; and one customer told him that his tomato felt like "a lead ball." His theory was that the added nutrients and "natural integrity" made the organic tomatoes so solid. He also reported that his tomatoes could sit on the kitchen table for weeks and "show no sign of decay," but he said the real proof was in the taste -- that the organic tomatoes were so sweet and juicy that customers kept coming back for more.

Talk with the kids about the farmer's story and ask whether they think it's true or not. Discuss the theory that the overuse of chemical fertilizers gets the tomatoes to grow quickly with water weight, as opposed to the organic tomatoes that are nourished with more real nutrients in the soil (leading to tomatoes that allegedly contain more vitamins and nutrients, as well). Organic proponents claim that an organic tomato will feel heavier and taste less watery than a conventionally grown tomato because of this.

To test this, head to the grocery store with your kids and buy a few conventional tomatoes. Then head to the farmers' market (or your own back yard, if you grow your own) and get some organic tomatoes of the same size (use a measuring tape to measure circumference).

Take them home and weigh them to see if they have the same weight. Also compare the color inside and finally, taste.

Making Fruit Leather -- In The Car

Summer time is the ideal time to make fruit leather. It puts fresh fruit to good use, especially over-ripe fruits that would otherwise go to waste. Make up a batch of fruit leather (our recipe involves blending fruit with a few drops of lemon juice and honey to taste, then pouring it about 1/8" thick onto a waxed paper lined cookie sheet to dry at very low heat until it's just barely tacky) and tell the kids you're going to "cook" it in the car!

Explain that you can dry fruit leather in a dehydrator or even a slow oven, but during the summer time many people use the insides of their cars as dehydrators because of the extreme temperatures inside.

Make up a batch or two and then spread it in cookie sheets and put it in the back window (be sure there are no flying bugs in the car or cover the pans with a window screen), preferably facing south.

Keep checking every few hours until they're done. It should take about an afternoon.

This is an excellent way to discuss how dangerous closed cars can be for children in the summer time. Talk about how much hotter it gets inside the car than outside. The kids can put a thermometer inside the car to see the temperature it reaches inside.

Heat Waves

We've all seen the rippling effect that extreme heat causes on the road, making it appear as if there's water up ahead, and the way the air seems to shimmer above a hot toaster.

This happens because the air around the heat source expands as it heats up. This makes the air less dense, so it begins to rise upwards. As light moves from the denser, cooler air to the less dense, hot air, it changes speed and is bent the way it would be by a lens. The rising hot air also swirls as it rises. As the air changes, the way that it bends the light also changes. This causes the light passing through the hot air to waver and shimmer.

Next time there's a heat wave in your town, head out to watch some heat waves with the kids and talk about the science behind them. If you can't find one outside, observe the toaster inside!

Ice Capades

Freeze a bunch of small treasures (natural or man-made) in a cake pan filled with water. Put it outside and let the kids work at freeing the tiny treasures with materials like salt, hot water and whatever else they dream up.

Encourage the kids to make predictions about what will free the treasures best and let them record the results, if they like.

Sprinkler Rainbows

It's easy enough to make a rainbow in your back yard sprinkler on a sunny day.

Turn on the sprinkler and stand so that the sun is at your back and look at the water. You should be able to see a rainbow in the water (finer mist works better).

Talk to the kids about why they can see the colors in the rainbow through the sprinkler.

The science behind rainbows: Rainbows are spectrums of light created when sunlight passes through water droplets in the atmosphere, caused by reflection and refraction (bending).All 7 colors of the visible spectrum that make up white light are present in rainbows. These are (in order) red, orange, yellow, green, blue, indigo and violet (most of us learned to think of ROY G BIV to remember the colors and their order).

Every person sees a rainbow in a slightly different way. A person standing next to you will see the rainbow in a slightly different place and when you move, the rainbow moves with you.

Try this: Have each person point to where they see the rainbow. Is everyone pointing at the exact same spot?

Summer Nature Sketches

Summer Nature Sketches

Summer Nature Projects & Observations

Summer Nature Projects & Observations

Autumn Nature Study Projects

Autumn is such a magical time of year for nature study. This is the perfect season for hikes and visits to state parks.

The changing seasons offer a wealth of opportunities to study leaves, trees, migration and more.

This is a time for harvesting back yard garden bounties and preserving foods for later.

If your family forages, look for wild edibles such as acorns (for acorn flour), chicken-of-the-woods mushrooms, apples and walnuts this time of year.

Here are some nature study projects well suited for autumn.

Amped Up Scavenger Hunt

Set up a scavenger hunt outside. This is a fun activity that can be tailored for all ages and can work in all kinds of subjects, too, to make it way more sophisticated than the standard nature hunts.

We generally tailor our hunts by each child's age to make it challenging and educational for all ages. We also include types of items we've learned about in our studies recently (such as rock types or edible plants).

Consider having the kids look for:

- Colors
- Things that start with certain letters
- Specific types of plants (such as deciduous trees or lichen)
- Specific varieties of plants (such as an elm tree or milkweed)
- Animal tracks
- Bird tracks
- Feathers
- Objects shaped like letters
- Types of birds

- Seed pods
- Something local Native Americans used for food or medicine
- Something early settlers used for food or medicine
- An edible plant
- A poisonous plant
- A plant that could be used as a natural dye
- An insect that's an herbivore
- An insect that's an ommivore
- Signs that an animal has been nearby
- A fossil
- A metamorphic rock

You can assign points for items, with more points for hard-to-find items. Kids can try to find as many as possible, or you can give easier lists and see if they can find them all.

Decide ahead of time if they should just spot the items and check them off, take pictures or gather items. Also be sure they don't gather items that are protected, dangerous or otherwise unwise.

Nature photography

Arm your child with a digital camera or cell phone with a good macro setting and head out to find wildflowers, insects, birds or other natural elements to photograph.

If you like, start a family blog of the photos and teach your child how to upload and caption the pictures. You'll sneak in science, art, computer skills, spelling, punctuation and more!

Paint Sample Match-Up

Collect some paint sample cards from your local paint department that have a variety of fall leaf colors, such as orange, brown and red.

Hand them out and have the kids attempt to find leaves that match as many colors on their cards as they can.

Fall Branch Preservation

Many people have preserved single autumn leaves through methods like pressing them between waxed paper or clear contact paper or dipping them in wax.

Here's a way to preserve a whole branch of fall leaves, and learn about how trees work while doing so.

You'll need:

- Small tree branches with colorful leaves
- Water
- Glycerin

Steps:

Select tree branches when leaves have first turned color.

Split the stems of the branches about three inches from the bottom and stand them in a bucket of warm water for several hours. Remove any leaves that are beginning to curl.

Prepare a solution of one part glycerin (available in the laxative section of most pharmacies) and two parts water.

Bring the solution to a boil, simmer gently

for 10 minutes, and remove it from heat and cool completely.

Cut the bottom of each branch at a sharp angle and stand the branches in the mixture and store in a cool, dark place until all the glycerin mixture has been absorbed, about 7-10 days.

You'll notice tiny beads of glycerin forming on the leaves. Wipe the leaves with a damp paper towel and dry thoroughly.

Your branches should be preserved at least over the fall, and they may last for several seasons.

Pumpkin Seed Lesson Plans

This is the time of year to scoop up pumpkins at super low prices. Not only can you cook the pumpkin for recipes (it's delicious in quick breads, soups, muffins and cakes, not to mention pies!) but the seeds are healthy, fun and useful for lots of fun activities with kids.

Here are a few ways to use the seeds in your homeschool...

Graphing: Give each child a piece of construction paper, a marker, a glue stick and a pile of pumpkin seeds.

Have the kids think up their own polling question (examples: What's your favorite season? Do you like pumpkin pie?), preferably with a limited number of possible answers.

Have them pose the question to friends and family (or you can post it on Facebook or message lists to get lots of answers quickly) and log the results.

Then have them make a bar chart of the answers, gluing pumpkin seeds to represent the numbers for each category.

Cooking: Kids can toast clean, dried pumpkin seeds and create their own delicious flavors. Have them toss 1 1/2 cups of pumpkin seeds with 2 tablespoons of melted butter or olive oil. Mix well, and then spread on a cookie sheet. Sprinkle liberally with seasonings, spices, salt and whatever they can dream up. Our kids have made up three flavors: garlic and salt, cajun (with salt and cajun seasoning) and a sweet mix of cinnamon, sugar, nutmeg and ground cloves. Bake at 300, stirring occasionally, for about 45 minutes or until light golden brown.

Math: Use pumpkin seeds for math manipulatives (to solve addition and subtraction problems, for instance) and to illustrate math concepts.

Challenge the kids to see how many ways they can divide 20 pumpkin seeds evenly (4x5, 2x10 and so on) and then try a prime number like 13.

You can also have them guess which numbers will have more piles -- 12 or 21? 6 or 7? 14 or 15?

It's a great way to illustrate factors and reinforce multiplication basics.

Art: Put pumpkin seeds in several disposable dishes and drizzle with tempera paint. Stir to coat and let dry in a single layer on waxed paper or another nonstick surface. Have the kids draw a simple picture on a piece of sturdy paper or cardstock, and then glue the colored seeds onto the picture.

Science: Grow pumpkin seeds in plastic baggies. Give each child a paper towel, a few pumpkin seeds and a ziplock bag. Have the kids dip the paper towel in water, gently squeeze out the excess and fold it to fit in bag. Place pumpkin seeds on top of the paper towel and seal the bag. Tape the bag to a sunny window or pin it to a bulletin board and check the seeds daily (add water to the bottom of the bag as needed, the paper towel will wick it up).

Pumpkin seeds can be fun for little ones too. Give toddlers a dish of seeds and several scoops and small cups. Pumpkin seeds are also fun in homemade playdough. They add a neat, bumpy texture when they're mixed in and are also fun to decorate on the top of playdough creations.

Leaf Tracking

Prepare for this activity by going on a walk around your neighborhood (or yard!) and collecting an assortment of distinct leaves. Head back and give your child the leaves with the task of finding the trees they came from.

This is trickier than it seems! You can bring a tree and leaf ID book to make it easier (and help your child pick up the names of many of your neighborhood trees).

Be sure to pick leaves that are different enough to distinguish from other varieties. You can also pick small clusters of berries and other parts of trees.

This is a great way to help kids learn botany and tree identification, and they will often notice very small differences in the leaves as they go on the quest.

Mashed Potato Science

The thing about homeschoolers is we find a way to make anything educational! Dinner time is no exception.

Teach your kids how to make mashed potatoes and talk about how science effects whether they're fluffy or gluey.

Explain that overcooked or insufficiently drained potatoes can become sticky, as can using the wrong kind of potato. The biggest reason that mashed potatoes get gluey, though, is being over-beaten.

Boiled potatoes develop swollen starch cells. When these cells are ruptured during mashing, they release starch. The more cells that are ruptured, the gummier the mashed potatoes. If you mash your potatoes with an electric mixer or (even worse) a food processor, too many cells will be be ruptured and you'll end up with "gluey" potatoes.

If you use a potato masher or put the potatoes through a ricer or food mill, these devices are gentler on the starch cells and you'll get fluffy, perfect potatoes.

Apple Orchard Visit

Most orchards offer tours for homeschool groups and families. At an orchard near our town, our family takes wagon rides, sees how the apples are washed on an assembly line, listens to stories, learns the proper way to pick apples and how to know when they're ready, and more. We always take home bags of apples to bake with and nibble.

More Apple Fun

There are lots of other ways to use apples for nature studies this time of year:

- Have a taste test of several different kinds of apples. Make predictions about how they will taste by color, size and other factors in advance.

- Put aside a slice of each type of apple and see if they all oxidize (turn brown from being exposed to oxygen) at the same rate. Make predictions ahead of time about which ones the kids think will brown fastest or brown the most. If you like, graph the results.

- Experiment with different substances such as lemon juice, lemon-lime soda and water to see if they will slow down or stop the apples' oxidation. Again, make predictions ahead of time, and graph the results if you like.

- Use apples for cooking and baking. Make homemade applesauce, apple muffins, apple pie and/or other apple dishes. How does cooking affect the apples' taste, texture and smell?

- Plant some apple seeds inside and see what happens.

- Cut apples in half and make nature prints by pressing the halves in tempera paint and stamping them on paper. Look at the designs and patterns they make. Also talk about symmetry and any other properties the kids notice in the apple prints.

Grape Harvesting

Are apples too predictable for your family? Why not try something different and visit a vineyard?!

One September, we picked our own grapes at a small family vineyard near our hometown. Not only did the kids have a wonderful time picking grapes, but they got to help crush them and strain the juice. We took home our own grape juice that we used to make the best tasting grape jelly we'd ever had (and we didn't even think we liked grape jelly!).

You can also look for wild grapes to harvest. These typically do not taste good raw (and can give you a stomach ache!) but they can make delicious jellies. Be sure to consult a foraging guide and make sure you correctly identify the grapes and have permission to gather them (if needed) before collecting them.

Nature Math

Make math manipulatives out of natural items outside.

Challenge the kids to help you collect all sorts of natural treasures to use for different number values.

You can use shells, rocks, pine cones, sticks (paint them and use different lengths like Cuisenaire rods!), tree nuts, you name it.

Put the kids in charge of deciding what each item is worth and then ask them to show you how to use them.

For instance, they could use shells like money (big ones are a dollar, little gray ones are five cents, and so on) and then "shop" with them.

Alternately, they could make base ten values for various items (these pine cones are 100, these rocks are 10, these seed pods are one...) and then use them for calculations.

Bendable Bones

If you're going to be having turkey this Thanksgiving, here's a great way to make use of those bones afterwards.

This simple science experiment teaches kids the importance of calcium -- and is also just really cool. We have a vegetarian Thanksgiving in our family but we have friends save some bones for us.

Here's what you need:

- A jar large enough to hold a chicken or turkey bone
- A chicken or turkey bone (legs or drumsticks work best)
- Vinegar

Here's what you do:

1. Remove any meat from the bone and rinse well in warm water.

2. Have the kids try to bend the bone and otherwise test its hardness.

3. Put the bone in the jar and cover it with vinegar. Put a lid on the jar and let it sit for three days.

4. Remove the bone from the jar, rinse and have the kids feel it now.

Here's what happened: Calcium is what keeps our bones hard. Vinegar is a mild acid, but it is strong enough to dissolve away the calcium in the bone. Once it dissolved the calcium in the bone, there was nothing to keep it hard and all that was left was soft bone tissue.

You can also add thinner bones to the vinegar and experiment with tying them in knots! If you want to try this experiment, look for some long, thin bones to add to the vinegar. Leave them for 3-4 days and then remove them and see if you can tie them in knots. Once they are exposed to the air for long enough, they'll harden again because they will react to the carbon dioxide in the air.

You can extend the lesson by talking about calcium. Foods rich in calcium include kale, spinach, soybeans, dairy products, white beans, bony fish such as sardines, okra, collards and calcium fortified foods like orange juice.

Be sure the kids also know that our bodies need vitamin D to absorb calcium and the best way to keep bones strong is to do lots of weight bearing exercise like walking. There's another benefit of those nature walks!

Migratory Bird Tracking

Many geese, ducks and other birds are flying south for the winter this time of year.

Set aside a time every day to watch for migrating birds and keep track of the numbers seen.

Write down the counts for each day, make predictions and/or graph the numbers.

Next year, see if you notice any changes in numbers, dates or patterns of migration.

Autumn Nature Sketches

Autumn Nature Sketches

Autumn Nature Projects & Observations

Autumn Nature Projects & Observations

Winter Nature Study Projects

Winter is a season for feeding the birds and watching the weather, helping outside animals and studying all of those natural materials you collected all through the year.

It's a great time to plan next year's garden and sprout things inside on window sills. It's also a perfect time for nature walks to look for animal tracks in the snow (or mud or sand).

If your family forages, this might be the season you're enjoying the frozen asparagus, dried elderberries, blueberry jam and other wild foods your family gathered together the rest of the year.

Here are some nature study projects well suited for winter.

Critter Buffet

Here's a fun way to help the birds and animals over the winter and also use them for some science fun.

Have the kids assemble a platter of various treats to offer the birds, squirrels and other back yard visitors. Encourage them to use a wide variety of types of foods -- seeds, nuts, fruit pieces, berries, etc.

Put the platter where your back yard visitors can come and sample it, hopefully near a window so you all can observe them as they visit.

Have the kids make predictions about which foods will be preferred by which critters. Which ones do they think will go first? See how accurate the predictions are.

"The Price Is Right" -- Temperature Style

Here's a fun challenge for the kids. Have each child guess the temperature outside and go see who's closest.

Take the math a step further by subtracting that temperature from the temperature inside to see how much warmer it is inside.

Also guess the temperature on the back porch, in the basement and in the refrigerator and freezer, and then see how close each person guessed.

Compare these temperatures to inside and outside temperatures.

This is a great opportunity for graphing, too. The kids can make bar graphs to show the temperatures of each of these areas.

Sun Tracking

The winter solstice is on December 21, which means the days will get to their shortest ever this month and then slowly start getting longer again after the 21st.

Track the times of the sunrise and sunset this month with the kids (either by observation or looking it up online or in the paper) and see just how much difference it makes from day to day.

Nature Abacus

Gather an assortment of natural materials such as shells, pine cones, rocks or seed pods and put them in rows of ten. Then show your child how to move the objects to solve math problems (for instance, for 132 + 44 you would move one in the hundreds, three in the tens and two in the ones, and then move four in the tens and four in the ones, for 176).

Also try subtraction and encourage kids to look for patterns and other ways to play with math with the objects.

Avocado Pit Pendants

Here's a simple, sweet nature craft that's free to make and as eco-friendly as they come! Avocado pit pendants are charming, personalized creations that are easy to create and surprisingly beautiful. Not only are avocados healthy and tasty, but they're in season in the winter, making them perfect materials for winter nature studies.

My homeschooling friend, Tiffany, showed me and my oldest girls how to make these charming pieces of art years ago. My daughters were instantly hooked, and we spent quite some time carving pendants and chatting.

Here's what you do.

1. Remove an avocado pit from the avocado and wash. You can use it right away or put it aside till later. It will stay soft enough to carve for about 2 weeks.

2. Have an adult use a sharp knife (such as a craft knife or steak knife) to slice the pit. It will be somewhat soft but be careful to protect your fingers. You can either slice the pit in half or into slices about 1/4" thick.

3. Remove the papery outer lining, which should peel right off at this point.

4. Use a pen knife or carving tool to carve a design into one side (or both) of the pendant. You can carve words, pictures, symbols or just a general design. If you like, you can also carve the pendant itself into a shape, such as a heart.

5. Use an awl or other sharp tool to push a hole into the top for hanging.

6. Attach a cord and wear!

As you wear the pendant, your natural oils will change the appearance of the pendant, giving it a glossy sort of wooden appearance. We haven't tried it, but we have heard you can also add jewels -- just carve out an opening, insert the jewel, and the pit will shrink as it hardens in order to encapsulate the gem.

Nature Center Field Trip

Winter is a perfect time to visit an area nature center and learn about native animals, do some bird watching, make some nature crafts and more. Many offer free classes, clubs and activities for all ages.

Also think of places outside of the box, in terms of nature visits. Our family frequently visits field offices of the Department of Natural Resources and similar sites, just to visit and see if they have any materials that would be useful for homeschooling. They often have educational materials such as posters, pamphlets and handouts. They are generally happy to answer questions or just chat about what they do and what sort of wildlife is in the area.

Cross Country Snow (Or Mud) Trek

If you live in a snowy climate, get out and enjoy the white stuff by going snow shoeing or cross-country skiing.

You can find affordable ski equipment at thrift stores or just go trekking in your winter boots.

While you're outside, look for animal tracks and see if you can identify them. You can find printable animal track ID cards and charts many places online.

If you're in a warmer climate, just head out for a nature walk, preferably somewhere that will show tracks well, like land that is muddy or has wet sand.

Tabletop Observation Garden

Winter is the perfect time to make a tabletop garden with root vegetables. Head to the store (or root cellar) and pick up some root vegetables like carrots, yams, parsnips, rutabagas and turnips. Try to pick veggies that have a little bit of green at the tops.

Cut about 2 inches off the top of each vegetable and stick three or four toothpicks near the very top of each. Set the toothpicks on the rim of a jar so the vegetables are suspended in them, and fill the jar with water so that the water level is above the bottom of each veggie.

Place the jars where they will get some natural light at least part of the day.

Check the veggies each day. Water as needed, to keep the bottoms submerged in water. Have the kids record observations about what happens.

You can also use different produce scraps to try to grow other plants. Pineapple tops, avocado pits and lettuce bottoms also make great experimental winter gardens.

Giant Ice Suncatchers

Kids can make a gorgeous, multi-colored ice wreath and then see how long it lasts before it melts. In some climates, this could be a matter of hours and in others, months!

Tint some water with different colors of food coloring and pour it in ice cube trays. Freeze until solid.

Fill a round cake pan or Bundt pan half full of clear water. Insert a paper cup that's filled with water in it to make a hole in the ice for hanging (not necessary if you use a Bundt pan).

Freeze for an hour and then drop in the colored ice cubes and return the pan to the freezer until fully frozen (the ice cubes will melt too much if the water is not already really cold in the pan).

When it's fully frozen, unmold it and pop out the cup. Tie some ribbon in the hole and hang outside. Voila!

Extend the educational value by having kids place bets on how long your ice wreath will last before melting.

Cloud Making

Here's one of those science experiments you can only do when you live where it gets very, very cold -- vaporize hot water!

If it gets bitterly cold where you live, you can throw boiling water into the air and it will instantly vaporize and turn into a cloud. This is one of those experiments that needs an adult doing most of the work and you need to use extreme caution.

Note that it needs to be extremely cold to make this work -- about -10°F (yes, that's ten degrees below zero). Some people report the experiment working up to 8°F above zero, but it's uncertain if it will work.

Here's what you do: Warm a flask up with boiling water, pour it out and then fill it again with boiling water (alternately, use a pan with a lid). Take the flask outside, pour a cup of the hot water and carefully throw it up into the air (watch for winds and be careful not to throw it on yourself or others!). A sweeping motion works best, as it disperses the water more and increases its surface area. This speeds the rate of evaporation.

As the 212°F water meets the cold, it should instantly vaporize, forming a cloud of steam that slowly drifts away and dissipates. Some of the droplets stay together and are instantly turned into small pieces of ice that fall to the ground.

What's happening? The rate of evaporation, the transition of water from the liquid phase to the gas phase, depends on the temperature difference between the water and the air. Hot water is already closer than cold water to evaporating, so the near-boiling water was already close to becoming a vapor, and the extreme temperature difference sped this up. The small water droplets also have a large surface area which allows for a great deal of evaporation, which removes the heat quickly. Also, the cooled droplets are so small that they can easily freeze in the super cold winter air. All of these reactions happen before the water hits the ground.

If it doesn't get cold enough where you live to do this experiment, you can watch videos of other people doing it on You-Tube.

The Clean Snow Experiment

This is a fun experiment to see if kids really should be eating that clean looking snow!

We came up with this idea one winter when we took a walk on a snowy day. The kids were scooping up handfuls of snow to eat. When I made a half-joking comment about eating pollution they assured me it was fine because they were only eating "clean snow."

I told them some groups like the Canadian Food Safety Institute have warned against eating snow because it is "a potential source of heavy metals, toxins, bacteria and viruses," particularly in urban areas. Scientists also talk about how snow literally cleans the pollutants from the air (by forming around pollutants, encapsulating them and falling to the ground), though they say that snow in rural areas is pretty safe.

I felt a science experiment coming on! We decided to see if we could find any pollutants.

One of the kids scooped up a jar of "clean" snow and filled another jar with tap water. She microwaved the snow to melt it and we all took a look. It looked pretty dirty!

I got a coffee filter and the kids helped pour the melted snow through it to see what sorts of things it would trap.

There was quite a lot of dirt, some things we couldn't identify, and something the kids guessed was a bug's leg or a very tiny animal hair.

Our kids were mildly annoyed but proclaimed that they were still going to eat fresh snow sometimes. They know about the hygiene hypothesis and I told them that was fine with me. I had already done research and had concluded on my own that I felt pretty safe with my kids eating our rural Minnesota snow. Still, it was fun and educational for them to do the research themselves in a way.

Here are some extensions for further experiments:

- Compare melted snow from two different locations, like from near a highway and from a wooded area.

- Put a jar outside to catch snow as it's falling and scoop up snow on the ground in another jar. Melt the snow in each and compare them.

- Look at melted snow under a microscope. Does it still look clean?

- Melt and strain some relatively clean, fresh snow and put it in a glass. Fill another glass with tap water and another with bottled water. Label them a, b and c. Can the kids tell which is which? Which tastes best?

Sound Studies

Head outside to different areas (such as the backyard, a nearby park and a shady spot down the street) several times a day and have the kids record every different source of noise (natural and man made) that they hear over a five minute period.

Ask questions ahead of time such as:

Do you think there will be more natural noises or man made noises in this site?

What time of day do you think there will be more natural noises?

What time of day do you think there will be more man made noises?

Do you think night time will be noisier or quieter for natural noises?

Do you think night time will be noisier or quieter for man made noises?

What day do you think will be noisiest?

How many noises do you think you'll hear?

Where do you think we'll hear the most natural noises?

If you like, graph the results with a bar graph or simple sticker chart.

Snow Volume

Fill a measuring cup with one cup of snow, then bring it inside and let it melt. See how much water it makes, subtract the difference, and talk about why snow takes up more volume than water.

You can expand on this by measuring different types of snow on different days.

Does fluffy, new snow take up more volume than snow that fell last week?

What about snow from a shoveled driveway?

You can also challenge the kids to see if they can pack the snow tightly enough to equal a full cup of snow once it's melted. Do they think they can do it?

If there's no snow where you live, try using a Slushie. Ask the kids if they think one cup of Slushie will still be one cup once it's melted.

Also see what happens if they freeze one cup of water.

Do they think it will still read exactly one cup on a measuring cup once it's frozen?

Winter Nature Sketches

Winter Nature Sketches

Winter Nature Projects & Observations

Winter Nature Projects & Observations

Yearly Nature Records

Bird Sightings

Species   Date   Location

Bird Sightings

Species   Date   Location

Animal Sightings

Species   Date   Location

Animal Sightings

Species   Date   Location

Garden/Foraging Records

Plants grown or gathered

Garden/Foraging Records

Plants grown or gathered

Made in the USA
Lexington, KY
07 March 2017